Bellingham

impressions

Photography and text by *Mark Turner*

FARCOUNTRY
PRESS

Left: Sculptor Robert McDermott created this bronze statue of "Dirty Dan" Harris—sailor, logger, rum runner, real estate developer, and Fairhaven founder. "Dirty Dan," who got his nickname from his reported poor personal hygiene habits, sits on a bench on the Fairhaven Village Green. Originally a separate town, Fairhaven joined the towns of Whatcom, Sehome, and New Whatcom to form Bellingham in 1903.

Facing page: Mount Baker, snowcapped year round by active glaciers, seems almost close enough to touch from the spectacular wildflower meadows on Skyline Divide. This popular day hike destination in the Mount Baker–Snoqualmie National Forest is on the northwest side of the 10,778-foot volcano. The flowers are a mix of blue lupines, yellow mountain arnica, and white American bistort and Sitka valerian.

Below: The Bellingham area has a nearly ideal climate for gardening. This Lummi Island home sits amid a lush garden, and a bicycle basket overflows with plants.

Front cover: In Whatcom Falls Park, Whatcom Creek meanders through areas of indigenous trees and shrubs before tumbling down Whatcom Falls.

Back cover: The Whatcom Museum of History and Art sits on a bluff overlooking Bellingham Bay.

Title page: Workers carved this tunnel, once part of Huntoon Drive, into Chuckanut sandstone on Sehome Hill in 1923. The road was closed in 1975 and the tunnel became part of the extensive trail system in what is now Sehome Hill Arboretum.

ISBN 10: 1-56037-466-7
ISBN 13: 978-1-56037-466-4

© 2007 by Farcountry Press
Photography © 2007 by Mark Turner

For more information about our books, write Farcountry Press, P.O. Box 5630, Helena, MT 59604; call (800) 821-3874; or visit www.farcountrypress.com.

Created, produced, and designed in the United States.
Printed in China.

12 11 10 09 08 07   1 2 3 4 5 6

Left: Fresh organic produce from Whatcom County farms is available each Saturday from April through December at the farmers' market on Railroad Avenue in downtown Bellingham. The early summer bounty here includes snap peas, onions, butterhead lettuce, and snow peas from Cedarville Farm.

Far left: Elizabeth Park, in the historic Columbia neighborhood, is the site of free weekly summer concerts sponsored by the Eldridge Society. Elizabeth Park is Bellingham's oldest park, created in 1884 on land donated by Captain Henry Roeder and later named for his wife, Mary Elizabeth. The current gazebo, built in 1984 for the one-hundredth anniversary of the park, is similar to the original 1901 gazebo.

Below: A western toad rests at the edge of Silver Lake. An adaptable amphibian, the western toad occupies a wide variety of habitats throughout western North America from British Columbia to northern Baja California and east to the western slopes of the Rocky Mountains.

Right: Roses highlight the corner garden of a stately Victorian home in historic Fairhaven.

Facing page: Nestled among the evergreens at Big Rock Garden Park, at the top of Alabama Hill in Bellingham, is this sculpture titled *Byron* by Tanya Kocinski. The park hosts an annual invitational sculpture exhibit and features more than thirty-five pieces in its permanent sculpture collection. In late spring, the park glows with rhododendron and azalea blossoms along its meandering paths.

Below: 'Pink Favorite' roses bloom in the Cornwall Park Rose Garden, a Bellingham city park at the corner of Cornwall Avenue and Illinois Street.

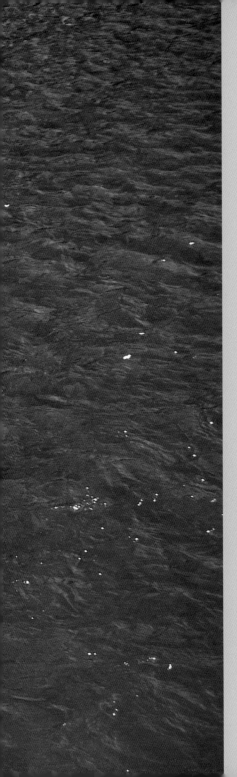

Above: *Phoebe*, a seventeen-foot-long Herreshoff Knockabout Sloop, is moored along the shore of Lake Whatcom.

Left: A fisherman casts for steelhead in the cold, clear waters of the Nooksack River. The steelhead trout spends part of its life cycle feeding in the ocean and, like salmon, returns to its freshwater birthplace to spawn.

Above, top: *Stone Enclosure: Rock Rings*, a sculpture by Nancy Holt, is one of many pieces in the Outdoor Sculpture Collection on the campus of Western Washington University.

Above, bottom: Competitors in the double bucking competition at the Deming Logging Show vie for a winning time, which requires teamwork and strength. Held the second full weekend of June each year, the logging show is a fundraiser for injured loggers and their families.

Right: The Wade King Student Recreation Center at Western Washington University features a rock climbing wall, three weight-lifting and cardio areas, basketball and volleyball courts, and a pool and whirlpool. The facility is named after a young Bellingham boy killed in the 1999 Whatcom Creek pipeline explosion and fire.

Left: Herring gulls often congregate in large flocks along the coast to scavenge and feed on fish and other prey. The bird can be recognized by its pink legs and the red spot on its large, yellow bill.

Below: Bellingham was once the home of one of the largest commercial fishing fleets on the west coast, but with overfishing and habitat losses, only a fraction of the former fleet is still active. This fishing net is stored in Squalicum Harbor, awaiting the next season.

Left: The Taylor Avenue dock and boardwalk are part of the South Bay Trail that connects downtown to Fairhaven. The original Taylor Avenue dock was built in the late 1800s. In 2004 the dock was refurbished and the boardwalk, which follows the route of an old railroad trestle over the bay, was constructed to fill a gap in the trail. It immediately became popular with walkers and cyclists and is a favorite place to watch the sun set.

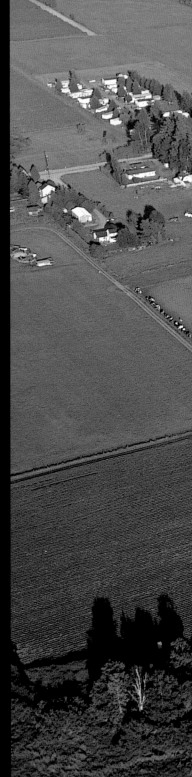

Above, top: Jonagold apples are the predominant variety grown commercially at several small orchards in Whatcom County.

Above, bottom: Black-and-white Holsteins are the most common breed of dairy cattle on Whatcom County farms. With more than 60,000 cows, the county is a major dairy producer and the nation's second-largest producer of powdered milk.

Right: Farming is a major business in Whatcom County, making it one of the top 100 agricultural counties in the nation. Rich soil, a mild climate, and adequate rainfall all contribute to Whatcom County's status as the nation's leading producer of raspberries and blueberries.

Left: This white Japanese chicken won first place in its class in the poultry competition at the Northwest Washington Fair in Lynden, which is held in August each year.

Facing page: Harris Avenue in historic Fairhaven is a quaint shopping area with many small specialty shops.

Below: Fairhaven Park, located on Chuckanut Drive just south of the Fairhaven business district, was created in 1906 and designed by John C. Olmstead. The park includes expansive lawns, a splash park, a playground, and an outdoor basketball court, as well as a small meeting room.

Good earth Pottery

ARTWOOD
MARKET & WINE

BANK

OPEN

Above: This small pond and wetland just a short hike from the Hannegan Pass Road is typical of such areas at low to middle elevation in Whatcom County. Insectivorous sundews grow on half-submerged logs. Frogs and salamanders lay their eggs in the shallow waters near the shore.

Facing page: Racehorse Creek Falls on an autumn day. An unmaintained trail off the North Fork Nooksack Road leads through a vine maple forest to this waterfall. Late spring to early fall is the best time to visit.

Above: A parade of massed pipe bands opens and closes events at the Bellingham Highland Games each June in Ferndale. The games also feature traditional Scottish athletic competitions, highland dancing, and piping competitions.

Left: The Whatcom Symphony Orchestra performs in the Mount Baker Theater. Built in 1927 as a vaudeville and silent movie house, the theater has been preserved and restored through a combination of public and private efforts. The ornate interior, in a Moorish-Spanish motif, seats about 1,500 patrons.

Above: A climber ascends out of a crevasse in the Coleman Glacier on Mount Baker during a practice session. Mount Baker is a popular ascent for mountaineers. Some of the crevasses, or cracks, in its glaciers appear to be nearly bottomless—an eerily beautiful icy-blue void best appreciated while firmly anchored from above. A fall can be fatal.

Above, right: A snowboarder passes through a gate in the Mount Baker Legendary Banked Slalom, the longest-running race in the history of snowboarding. The event attracts world-class professionals and local amateurs, who ride the same challenging natural halfpipe course. The Mount Baker Ski Area was one of the first to welcome snowboarders, and it continues to be a popular destination for the sport.

Facing page: Two climbers make their way along a steep slope near the summit of Goat Mountain on a rare clear winter day, with Mount Baker on the horizon behind them. The North Cascades are the most glaciated and remote mountains in the lower forty-eight states, attracting climbers from around the world to their rugged peaks.

WHATCOM COUNTY COURTHOUSE

311

Above: A Douglas squirrel raids a backyard birdfeeder. This small native species is common in forests west of the Cascades, but it is more often heard—scolding and chirping from the treetops—than seen. They typically feed on conifer seeds, which they gather by dropping cones to the ground, often hoarding them for winter food.

Right: Lavender and lamb's ears line a brick path winding through part of the Tennant Lake Fragrance Garden near Ferndale, where visitors are encouraged to touch and smell the flowers. This county park also has an interpretive center, an observation tower, and an extensive wetland accessible by a raised boardwalk.

Facing page: The Whatcom County Courthouse in Bellingham's civic center. Approximately 184,000 people live in the county, and this building is the seat of the government. On election nights, vote-watchers gather in the rotunda to catch the latest poll results.

Above: A sea kayaker nears the finish line of the annual Ski to Sea race. The final leg of the race takes place on Bellingham Bay from Squalicum Harbor to Marine Park. Sea kayaking is a popular sport on the protected inland marine waters around Bellingham and the nearby San Juan Islands, which have hundreds of miles of shoreline to explore and numerous places to camp.

Right: The sidewalks of downtown Bellingham come alive with art each August during the Allied Arts Chalk Art Festival. Artists of all ages create colorful, but ephemeral, masterpieces.

PHOTO BY MARK FULLER

Above: These mouth-watering, freshly picked blueberries are just one example of the wide variety of crops Whatcom County produces. The fertile farmland north of Bellingham is one of the nation's largest producers of blueberries.

Right: A full moon hangs over the placid South Fork Nooksack River on a summer evening. The South Fork is a popular summer float trip, drawing many local folks with inner tubes who start near Acme and float downstream.

Above: A bald eagle, perched high above a stream, keeps a watchful eye out for prey in the river below. The North Fork Nooksack River draws a large concentration of bald eagles each winter, where they feed on chum salmon from late December to early February. Popular places to view them are the Deming Eagle Homestead Park, the Mosquito Lake Road bridge, and the North Fork Nooksack Road.

Left: The annual Ski to Sea Grand Parade, held Saturday of Memorial Day weekend, features many high school bands, dozens of floats and marching units, and thousands of spectators lining the streets of downtown Bellingham. Here the Marysville Pilchuck High School band marches past Assumption Catholic Church on Cornwall Avenue.

Facing page: Opened in 2006, the Depot Market Square on Railroad Avenue is the home of Bellingham's weekly farmers' market. The building won an American Institute of Architects Northwest Washington Citation Award and was designed to call to mind the railroad station that once stood nearby.

Above: Ochre sea stars cling to rocks at low tide in Larrabee State Park. These sea stars are common in the low to mid-intertidal zones on rocky shores and feed primarily on mussels. They grow to about 10 inches across and range in color from orange to brown to purple.

Right: Nooksack Falls, about 40 miles east of Bellingham on Mount Baker Highway, plunges more than 100 feet over a rocky precipice. A fenced vista point allows for safe viewing.

Left: Mushrooms and a lush carpet of mosses blanket the forest floor of most lower elevation forests in the Pacific Northwest.

Right: Old Main, constructed between 1896 and 1914, is the original building on the campus of Western Washington University. Until 1928 it housed the entire Normal School, as it was originally known. *The Man Who Used to Hunt Cougars for Bounty* was sculpted on site of granite in 1972 by Richard Beyer and is part of WWU's extensive outdoor sculpture collection.

Below: Black-tailed deer are common and can be a garden pest in many Bellingham neighborhoods, where they find hostas and roses to be tasty treats that complement their natural forage.

Fishermen's memorial *Safe Return* in Zuanich Point Park at Squalicum Harbor was placed "in memory of those who have gone to sea in pursuit of their livelihood, never to return." It is silhouetted here as the sun drops behind Lummi Island.

Left: Large murals appear on several of Bellingham's downtown buildings. This one, which celebrates fresh food and outdoor recreation, is adjacent to the entrance to the Bellingham Community Food Co-op and was painted by local artist Karen Theusen.

Facing page: The Marine Life Center at Squalicum Harbor is a good place to learn about life in the marine waters just off shore from Bellingham. Here a family observes giant green sea anemones and other sea animals in the observation tank. The Marine Life Center also has several smaller aquariums and a touch tank.

Below: Mountain biking, one leg of the Ski to Sea relay race, is popular on trails in and around Bellingham. Galbraith Mountain, where mountain bikers have worked together to build and maintain a network of trails, draws riders from near and far. Other well-loved trails are on Chuckanut and Blanchard mountains south of town.

Left: The Procession of the Species Parade, held the first Saturday in May, celebrates community, creativity, and connections with nature. This large sun puppet is leading the parade through Bellingham's civic center.

Facing page: The triangular Flatiron Building was constructed of reinforced concrete in 1908 for the Bellingham Bay Furniture Company, which occupied it until 1978. It received Federal Landmark status in 1983.

Below: Chuckanut Drive was the first road connecting Bellingham and the Skagit Valley to the south. Designated a National Scenic Byway, the narrow, curving road features several vista points where drivers can pull over and enjoy the view of the San Juan Islands. The road also passes Larrabee State Park, Washington's first.

Above: Chuckanut sandstone, exposed on the rocky shoreline just south of Bellingham, erodes to form exotic shapes and textures. Larrabee State Park is a good place to explore the shoreline; tidepools often contain sea stars and anemones.

Right: Mount Baker is visible from much of Bellingham and northern Whatcom County, standing sentinel on the skyline. At sunrise, it is silhouetted above dairy cows grazing in a mist-shrouded pasture.

Above: Several Whatcom County farms have "you pick" strawberry fields where you can gather the very freshest Puget Reliant or Shuksan strawberries each June.

Left: Peace Arch State and Provincial Parks, spanning the Canadian border at the Blaine border crossing, feature this large floral American flag on one end and a Canadian flag at the other. The park hosts an annual outdoor sculpture exhibit each summer and has several picnic areas on both sides of the border. The floral flags can be seen when driving through the border crossing on Interstate 5, which becomes Highway 99 in Canada.

Above: The American Museum of Radio and Electricity, in the downtown cultural district, houses one of the most extensive collections of early radios—more than 800—and other objects tracing the historic exploration of electricity. The museum has interactive exhibits and a fully operational low-power FM station that can also be heard on the internet (www.amre.us).

Facing page, top: Boys and girls, ages 13 and under, paddle eleven-man racing canoes in the junior buckskins category of the Lummi Stommish canoe race. The races help carry on the long tradition of coastal canoeing by the Native American tribes that have lived here for centuries. The Lummi Nation and the Nooksack Indian Tribe both have reservations in Whatcom County.

Facing page, bottom: The canoe leg of the Ski to Sea race follows the Nooksack River from Everson to Ferndale.

Old-growth Northwest forests feature immense Douglas-firs that can reach up to 8 feet in diameter, such as this one growing near Mount Baker Highway. Douglas-fir trees typically live more than 400 years; if undisturbed by fire or windthrow, they can live more than 1,200 years. The area now occupied by Bellingham was originally covered by forests like this one, which also includes western hemlock and western red cedar.

Above: The Heather Meadows Visitor Center is buried under up to 30 feet of snow each winter. It was built by the Civilian Conservation Corps (CCC) in 1940 as the Austin Pass Warming Hut. In the summer, it houses interpretive displays and is the starting point for several trails that explore the geology and plant life of the Heather Meadows area, located adjacent to the Mount Baker Ski Area near the end of Mount Baker Highway.

Right: Great blue herons are relatively common along streams and the coast throughout the Pacific Northwest. These large birds, with a wingspan up to 6 feet, feed on fish and small mammals.

Far right: The stone bridge over Whatcom Creek just below Whatcom Falls was built by the CCC in 1939 and is a must-see year round for visitors and residents alike. The falls are the centerpiece of 241-acre Whatcom Falls Park, which has an extensive network of trails, a fish hatchery, and a fishing pond exclusively for youth under 16.

Above: This stone bench provides a place to rest along the 3-mile loop trail through the Stimpson Family Nature Reserve, located along Lake Louise Road near Lake Whatcom. The park, which was acquired by the Whatcom Land Trust, is a place to learn about and enjoy old-growth and multiple-age forest stands, and also features a large wetland.

Left: Workers harvest fresh zucchini squash at Cedarville Farm, one of several small farms providing fresh produce to local stores, the farmers' market, and direct to families through Community Supported Agriculture.

Facing page: The Tennant Lake Fragrance Garden near Ferndale has more than 200 species of herbs and other fragrant plants in wheelchair-accessible raised beds with braille labels. Visitors are encouraged to touch and smell the plants. Interpretive signs discuss sustainable and drought-tolerant gardening practices. This view is from atop the 50-foot-tall observation tower nearby.

Above: The *Bellingham Herald* building, built in 1926, is a downtown landmark on the corner of State and Chestnut streets.

Facing page: Mount Shuksan, practically in Bellingham's back yard, is one of the most photographed mountains in the world. In autumn, Cascades blueberries around Picture Lake color the ground red, contrasting with subalpine firs, mountain hemlocks, and the brilliant white glaciers slowly creeping down from the mountain's summit.

Above: Bellingham is the southern terminus for the Alaska Marine Highway System. Catch an Alaska Ferry at the Bellingham Cruise Terminal and sail up the inside passage to Haines and beyond. Ferries arrive and depart Bellingham weekly year round and twice weekly during the peak summer season.

Left: Anglers flock to the mouth of Whatcom Creek in winter to catch chum salmon that pass through from the ocean, resting here before climbing the waterfall that provided power for the first lumber mill built on Bellingham Bay. The area, while still industrial, is undergoing a transition. The former Georgia-Pacific pulp mill, adjacent to the tissue mill steaming in the background, has closed and the property will be redeveloped. Maritime Heritage Park, which spans both sides of the creek, was once a garbage dump and sewage treatment plant; it now houses a fish hatchery.

Above: Nothing says Whatcom County agriculture better than baskets of fresh red raspberries. More raspberries are grown and processed here than in any other county in the United States.

Right: Blueberries are another important Whatcom County crop, popular with locals who visit farms to pick their own fresh fruit each summer.

Facing page: McPhail Farms, near Lynden, hosts a raspberry festival each June and grows eight varieties of berries for you-pick customers.

From the summit of Winchester Peak, the old Winchester Fire Lookout provides a 360-degree panoramic view of the North Cascades. The view here is to the north, with Canadian Border and American Border peaks, Mount Larrabee, and the Pleides from left to right along the ridge. If you were to turn around you'd see Goat Mountain, Mount Shuksan, and Mount Baker, with Twin Lakes just below.

Above, top: Lynden Youth Klompen Dancers dance in their wooden shoes around the May Pole in Lynden's annual Holland Days Parade of Provinces. Lynden has a strong Dutch influence as a result of extensive immigration following World War II.

Above, bottom: Dancers in the Lummi Stommish Powwow junior boys traditional dance competition wear colorful traditional costumes. The Stommish Powwow honors military veterans and is an annual gathering where Lummis and members of other Northwest Native American tribes join in renewing old friendships, making new ones, singing, and dancing. There are also canoe races, games, and a salmon barbeque.

Left: Scouts and members of other youth groups from the U.S. and Canada march through the Peace Arch at the Blaine border crossing during the annual Hands Across the Border celebration in June. Built in 1921, the Peace Arch represents the longest undefended border in the world and is the first monument dedicated to world peace.

Above: Blanchard Mountain, south of Bellingham above Chuckanut Drive, is a popular launch point for hang gliders who can ride the thermals for hours before landing on the Skagit Flats more than 1,200 feet below.

Right: Double-crested cormorants perch on old pilings at the end of Semiahmoo Spit in Blaine. Once the site of a huge salmon cannery, the narrow spit between Drayton Harbor and Boundary Bay is now home to Semiahmoo Resort. It is a good place to go bird watching.

Far right: The Bellingham Yacht Club sponsors several sailing regattas on Bellingham Bay. Boulevard Park provides a convenient place to watch the action.

Left: This Lummi totem pole, carved by Jewell James, was erected in Maritime Heritage Park in 1997. Titled *Story of Salmon Woman,* it tells a conservation story featuring Raven, Salmon Woman, and Bear. It was commissioned by the Nooksack Salmon Enhancement Association, which is working to restore wild salmon runs in Whatcom County streams.

Facing page: The Bellingham Children's Museum is full of interactive exhibits that encourage children ages two to eight to explore and learn. The giant octopus and its cave are part of By the Bay: Working on the Waterfront, one of many changing exhibits.

Below: Peas hang on the vine, ready to be picked and delivered to the farmers' market.

Above: Skyviewing *Sculpture,* sculpted by Isamu Noguchi and installed on Red Square in 1969, is one of the best-known pieces in Western Washington University's outdoor sculpture collection.

Left: The Fairhaven Village Green, located behind Village Books and the Colophon Cafe, has covered pergolas for the Wednesday farmers' market in the summer—and other events year-round. Outdoor movies are shown on the green on summer nights.

Above: Dozens of hardy souls celebrate New Year's Day by plunging into Birch Bay. Plungers get to warm up afterwards with hot beverages.

Right: Youngsters learn basic sailing skills in small boats on Lake Padden in classes offered by the Bellingham Yacht Club.

Facing page: The annual Ski to Sea race gets underway with the mass start of some 400 cross-country skiers at the Mount Baker Ski Area. After skiing an up- and downhill figure-8 loop, the cross-country skiers hand off to downhill skiers. The race works its way down to sea level, in five additional legs: running 8 miles, road biking 36 miles, canoeing 18 miles, mountain biking 9 miles, and sea kayaking 5 miles.

Above: Pioneer Park in Ferndale is home to one of the best collections of pioneer buildings in the Northwest. Each July the Old Settler's Picnic is held in the park, a time to share stories and visit friends.

Facing page: The Whatcom Museum of History and Art, housed in Bellingham's 1892 City Hall and three adjacent buildings, features exhibitions of contemporary art and regional history. It holds more than 200,000 artifacts of regional importance, including an extensive photographic archive.

Above: Lairmont Manor, in the Edgemoor neighborhood, was completed in 1916 for the family of Charles Xavier Larrabee, founder of the Fairhaven Land Company and benefactor of Fairhaven Park and Larrabee State Park. On the National Register of Historic Places, Lairmont is now owned by a non-profit organization and available for weddings and other events.

Facing page: The Port of Bellingham has landscaped the Squalicum Harbor Promenade with colorful flowers and waving grasses. The 2.5-mile paved walkway around the harbor connects Bellwether on the Bay with Zuanich Point Park and is popular with walkers, bicyclists, and joggers.

A variety of watercraft are moored in Squalicum Harbor on the Bellingham waterfront on a calm summer evening.

Above: Dirty Dan Days, the last weekend in April, celebrates Fairhaven's founder, "Dirty Dan" Harris, and the community's history. Pictured are the winner of the Dirty Dan look-alike contest and one of the "ladies of the night." The day-long celebration also includes a chowder cook-off, music, and a piano race.

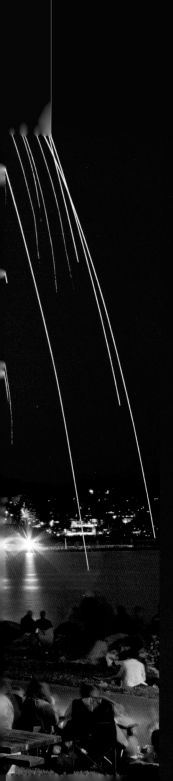

Left: Fourth of July fireworks burst over Bellingham Bay, seen here from Zuanich Point Park.

MARK TURNER has been photographing the Pacific Northwest since he moved to Bellingham in 1990. He was drawn to the natural beauty of the mountains and coast and has explored the area extensively as a hiker, backpacker, and climber—often with many pounds of camera gear on his back. Mark is a freelance editorial photographer specializing in botanical subjects, especially Northwest wildflowers and gardens. Photographing community events, festivals, landmarks, and architecture is a welcome and rewarding change of pace for Mark. *Wildflowers of the Pacific Northwest*, which he photographed, won an American Horticultural Society Book Award in 2007. View more of Mark Turner's photography at www.turnerphotographics.com.